Hi there!

I'm so glad that you could come with me on my very special Bible adventure. Together we will go back in time . . . back long ago to hair-raising battles, bad kings and good kings, violent earthquakes, giants, plus much more! These adventures are even more exciting because they really happened. In fact, you can look them up for yourself in the Bible, God's Holy Word written just for you. With every new adventure, the Bible book, chapter, and verses are given . . . be sure to ask a grown-up to help you find them.

One more thing: As you enter each new adventure, see if you can find me, Rupert. I brought along my pet bluebird, Reginald, but he never seems to stay with me. Where can he be? If you find him, let me know. Have fun, and don't get lost!

Rupert

THE FUN BIBLE SEARCH BOOK
...FIND RUPERT

CHAD FRYE

To My Blessed Mother
Barbara L. Frye
A Wonderful Example of the Proverbs 31 Woman

A BARBOUR BOOK

THE TEN PLAGUES
EXODUS 6:29–12:36

Once the Israelite people were held as slaves in Egypt. God sent Moses and Aaron to tell Pharaoh, the ruler of Egypt, to let the Israelites go free. Pharaoh would not, so God sent ten plagues – such troubles as frogs, lice, flies, locusts, and darkness, to name five – to cover the land of Egypt and convince Pharaoh. After the tenth plague, Pharaoh had had enough!

Find Rupert, Reginald, and things highlighted below.

Beach ball

Sick bull

Shot

Cowboy

Aaron

Baby

Moses

Pail

GIDEON

JUDGES 6–7

For seven years at harvest time the evil Midianites had stormed into Israel and carried away all of the Israelites' food. God chose a brave man, Gideon, to destroy the Midianites. With just three hundred men of courage, Gideon surrounded the camp of the Midianites in the middle of the night. Suddenly they shouted, "The sword of the Lord and of Gideon," and blew their trumpets. The Midianites were no longer a problem for Israel.

Find Rupert, Reginald, and things highlighted below.

Pea shooter

Arrow in apple

Gideon

Colored blanket

White flag

Bugle

Teddy bear

SAMSON
JUDGES 13–16

Samson was a very strong man because God gave him power. (The secret of Samson's strength was his long hair.) Samson was so strong that he once killed a lion with his bare hands! Because Samson disobeyed God, God let the Philistines cut his hair and he became weak. Samson was then captured by the Philistines and made blind. At a great feast held in the Philistines' temple, God restored Samson's strength one last time. Samson pulled down the pillars of the temple, killing all who were there, and saved the Israelites from the Philistines.

Find Rupert, Reginald, and things highlighted below.

Kid licking Icing

Pie

Love bird

Tight squeeze

Ham

Sad boy

Blindfold

PIN THE HAIR ON SAMSON

DAVID & GOLIATH
1 SAMUEL 17

The Israelites and the Philistines were at war. King Saul of Israel had a problem and his name was Goliath. The Philistines' not-so-secret weapon, Goliath stood nine feet tall, wore armor head to foot, and carried a spear twice as long and heavy as any other man could hold. When Goliath challenged Israel's army to fight him, David, a shepherd boy, armed with just a sling and five stones — and the power of God — killed the mighty giant and sent the Philistines running.

Find Rupert, Reginald, and things highlighted below.

Barber

Turtle

Teapot

Saul's armor

Programs

Hungry dog

KING SOLOMON'S TEMPLE 1 KINGS 5–8

King David had always wanted to build a temple for God, but God had other plans. When Solomon, David's son, became king, the time was right. King Solomon built a beautiful temple to God on Mount Moriah out of stone, cedar trees, and gold. Seven years were spent building the temple, and when it was done Solomon dedicated it to the Lord.

Find Rupert, Reginald, and things highlighted below.

Bird bath

Boy sliding

Tickling

Solomon

Falling coconut

Thin rope

SHEWBREAD

967 BC

JACHIN

BOAZ

GOLD

Lebanon Farms CEDAR WOOD FROM THE MIDDLE EAST

QUEEN JEZEBEL

1 KINGS 18–19:2; 21
2 KINGS 9:20–37

Queen Jezebel, the wife of King Ahab of Israel, was an evil woman. Jezebel worshiped Baal and wanted to destroy the prophets of the one true God. Elijah, a great prophet of the Lord, came from the desert to get rid of Baal. Eventually God killed Jezebel for her wickedness.

Find Rupert, Reginald, and things highlighted below.

Armor

Jezebel

Baseball glove

Salesman

Bird into window

Crowbar

White pigeon

QUEEN ESTHER

THE BOOK OF ESTHER

For his new queen King Ahasuerus chose a beautiful Jewish girl named Esther who lived with her cousin, Mordecai. Shortly after Esther became queen a wicked man named Haman rose in power in the king's court and earned many favors. Haman gave an order, without telling the king, that all Jews should be killed, including Mordecai. When Esther learned of this plan through her cousin, she saved the lives of Mordecai and her people and Haman was hanged (in place of Mordecai) for his evil trickery.

Find Rupert, Reginald, and things highlighted below.

Esther

Fruit bowl

Tattoo

Mordecai

Falling flowers

Thermos

Lawn mower

Haman

THE GARDEN OF GETHSEMANE

MATTHEW 26:1–57

At the Last Supper Jesus said that one of His twelve Apostles sitting at the table would betray Him. (To "betray" means to turn over an innocent person to an enemy, or to be a traitor.) Later, when Jesus and His Apostles were in the Garden of Gethsemane, one of the twelve, Judas Iscariot, who had been paid thirty pieces of silver to betray Jesus, came with many soldiers to take Jesus away. Jesus Christ, the Son of God, went away quietly to die for the sins of all of us.

Find Rupert, Reginald, and things highlighted below.

Owl

Bull's-eye

Judas Iscariot

Shaving soldier

Club

Sideburns

THE POOL OF BETHESDA

JOHN 5:2–18

The Pool of Bethesda was a place where great crowds of sick, blind, and handicapped people gathered to be healed by the rising and bubbling of the waters. You could only be healed at those times when the water reached a certain level. Once when Jesus visited the pool He noticed a lame man who could not reach the waters in time. Jesus performed a miracle by healing the man.

Find Rupert, Reginald, and things highlighted below.

Naked sheep

Three-legged man

Blue man

Vulture

Christ healing lame man

Blind man

UNCLEAN

Pool of BETHESDA

LAZARUS

JOHN 11:1–46

Lazarus was Jesus' good friend. He became sick one day. Mary and Martha, the sisters of Lazarus, sent for Jesus. When Jesus received word about Lazarus, He did not hurry, but instead arrived after Lazarus had died and been buried in the tomb four days. When Jesus arrived at Lazarus's tomb, He called to Lazarus to come out . . . and Lazarus did! As a result of this miracle, many people believed in Jesus Christ.

Find Rupert, Reginald, and things highlighted below.

Small-horned goat

Cactus

Lobster

Harpoon

Scroll

Cymbals

Big ears

WAILERS
LOCAL
#217

THE PHILIPPIAN JAILOR ACTS 16:12–40

Once when Paul and Silas, Jesus' followers, came to the city of Philippi they caused an evil spirit to come out of a slave girl who was a fortune teller. Her angry masters, who needed the money from her fortunes, had Paul and Silas sent to jail. Around midnight, while Paul and Silas were singing hymns and praying, an earthquake shook the walls of the jail freeing all the prisoners. The jailor was so happy that none of the prisoners escaped he became a Christian that night and was baptized by Paul and Silas.

Find Rupert, Reginald, and things highlighted below.

Thief

Paul

Curlers

Soldier under shield

Slipper

Teddy bear

Bulging eyes

MARS' HILL

ACTS 17:15–34

When Jesus' follower, Paul, was in Athens, Greece, he saw that the people worshiped many idols, even an idol "to the unknown God." The people took Paul to a temple on Mars' Hill where he told all about "The Unknown God," Jesus Christ. Some doubted Paul, but others believed.

Find Rupert, Reginald, and things highlighted below.

Patches

Mask & snorkel

Hammer & chisel

Nightmare

Diamond headband

Ice cream

Wheelbarrow

What other things can you find?

TEN PLAGUES

1. Frogs in love
2. Six cats
3. Sharks
4. Farmer
5. Addition problem
6. Thermometer
7. The ten plagues
8. Fly swatter
9. Tackle box

GIDEON

1. Fire arrow
2. Man with three horns
3. Karate
4. Israelites without a torch
5. Knife throwing
6. Duelers
7. Shadows
8. Two axes

SAMSON

1. Wiener roast
2. Cracked pot
3. Man in pain
4. Jumping fish
5. Footless shoe
6. Mouse
7. Twisted twister
8. Banana peel
9. Tipping a waiter
10. Human hog

DAVID & GOLIATH

1. Twins
2. Backwards "R"
3. Outhouse
4. Periscope
5. Rude awakening
6. Flag burning
7. Reversed tent flaps
8. Little guy with big helmet
9. Man sharpening sword
10. Checker game
11. Blinds
12. Cheerleaders

SOLOMON'S TEMPLE

1. Man digging
2. Armored wagon
3. Sewing machine
4. Time clock
5. Charging bull
6. Tic-tac-toe
7. Golden footprints
8. Clipboard
9. Yo-yo

JEZEBEL

1. Skylight
2. Raccoons
3. Ants
4. Mail carrier
5. Long dachshund
6. Barbecue
7. Man whistling
8. Hose
9. Christmas tree